Ephesians

Experience God's Power

Sarah K. Howley

Flaming Dove Press

Ephesians: Experience God's Power

Copyright © 2024 Sarah K. Howley

Flaming Dove Press
an imprint of
InspiritEncourage LLC
1520 Belle View Blvd #5081
Alexandria, VA 22307
www.inspiritencourage.com

All Scripture quotations, unless otherwise indicated, are taken from the Holy Bible, New International Version®, NIV®. Copyright © 1973, 1978, 1984, 2011 by Biblica, Inc.® Used by permission of Zondervan. All rights reserved worldwide. www.zondervan.com. The "NIV" and "New International Version" are trademarks registered in the United States Patent and Trademark Office by Biblica, Inc.®

ISBN 978-1-960793-16-4 (e-pub)
ISBN 978-1-960793-17-1 (paperback)
ISBN 978-1-960793-18-8 (large print)

Printed in the United States of America

Library of Congress Control Number: 2024925627

Contents

Welcome

The letter to the Ephesians is attributed to Paul and likely written under Roman guard, as described in Acts 28. The city of Ephesus was a "mixed salad" of cultures, as one of the largest trading cities in the Roman empire. This multiculturalism, multi-belief-ism, was the background of Paul's teachings to the Ephesians through the lens of his heritage. As Paul called himself "a Hebrew of Hebrews" (Phil. 3:5), it offered a solid Judeo-Christian theological perspective on the multicultural congregation of the thriving city.

This letter to the Ephesians is often viewed as offering a perspective of depth and practicality in the walk with Christ as our Lord. The first three chapters remind readers of who and what they are as well as the gifts bestowed upon them as followers of Christ. The last three chapters remind readers of what and how they should live and are full of instructions and practical insights about living out life in Christ. The epistle's comparison of Gentile and Christian life throughout offers the opportunity to understand the consistent message of the Bible, from the Old Testament to the New.

As modern-day believers, we were likely not instructed in the Hebrew way of life or Scriptures as Paul and many of his hearers or readers were. As such, there are a great many passages from the Old Testament which could enrich our understanding of the Christian life. This study sets out to highlight some of those passages to mine the depth of Paul's words and instruction for Christians today.

Each session opens with warm-up introductory questions, goes on to a reading from Ephesians and questions related to the passage. Then the study includes Old Testament passages which are tied to the session's reading, as well as questions. Each study session ends with considerations for personal application. Additional tips and suggestions on approaching the study for individuals and groups follow.

Suggestions for Study

This study is composed of 8 sessions and is designed for individual or small group study. It is written to foster thought and discussion of the scripture, encouraging individuals and groups seeking God to have conversations about the text. For 'You will seek me and find me when you seek me with all your heart,' as Jeremiah 29:13 says.

General Guidelines for Individual Study

1. Open each session with prayer. Ask God to speak through his Word.

2. Respond to the Introduction questions to focus on the theme of the session and what the Bible says in the main reading.

3. Read the passage more than once. Using different translations can offer expanded viewpoints on the meaning of the original text. This study uses the New International Version (NIV) as the basis of questions and quotes. However, any version may be used to provide insight and assist in revealing meaning.

4. This study is designed to offer a starting point for the discovery of what God has to say to you through his Word. Because the study looks at how the Old Testament is reflected in the epistles, there are observation and interpretation questions about the readings in Ephesians and then about the links in the Old Testament, as well as comparisons between the passages. These are followed by application questions for personal and group discussion. Writing your responses will provide clarity and focus your thoughts on the verses.

5. Use a Bible dictionary or other reference books to look up any unfamiliar words, places, or names.

General Guidelines for Group Study

1. Come to sessions prepared. Some groups will choose to read and respond ahead of time then gather and discuss together; others will gather to read and discuss together. Before beginning, agree how you would like to proceed so all are prepared.

2. Be an active participant in the group by sharing your thoughts and responses to the questions. Groups often have members who are of varied maturity in Christ and each perspective should be valued.

3. Listen to each other. Consider the amount of time that is available for all to share and be careful not to dominate the conversation.

4. Be open. As there are various 'right' answers, be open to considering alternate viewpoints and agree to disagree.

5. Maintain confidentiality of the group. For participants to be willing to share and grow, the trust level in the group must be high. Do not share outside the group unless permission is given to do so.

6. Expect God to meet you in the study. His Word is living and active (Heb. 4:12) and he is present when we gather in his name (Matt. 18:20).

Introduction

Paul addressed some of the "big ideas" of Christianity in his
letter to the Ephesians. From grace and new life to unity and
blessings, Paul wanted his readers to understand what life in
Christ encompasses. As you begin the study, what "big ideas" of
Christianity are you already familiar with?

The city of Ephesus was a thriving trade city on the coast
of modern-day Turkey when Paul wrote his letter. It was a
multicultural location where many worshiped other gods; there
was even a temple of Artemis nearby. Paul wrote in part to
remind the Ephesians how they were different from people who
worshiped other gods. Take a moment to note down what you
would tell someone is different about you because you worship
God and not gods.

Session 1: Spiritual Blessings in Christ

Ephesians 1:1-23

Opening

What does "blessing" mean to you? Name three blessings that you have received this week.

List three people who are a blessing to you and write down the reasons.

Paul opened his letter to Ephesians with a reminder of who they are in Christ and the glorious nature of Christ himself. Chosen, adopted, given an inheritance, all of the ideas that Paul used in the opening of this letter bring to mind an inestimable value of the person. Not only the people of Ephesians, but all followers who come today are of inestimable value to Christ and the kingdom of God.

Read Ephesians 1:1-23.

Reading Questions

Paul calls the Ephesians holy at the beginning of the letter. How were they holy or what did it mean for the people in Ephesus to be holy?

What did God choose the Ephesians for?

Paul revealed the mystery described in verse 9; what was it?

What was the seal that marked the Ephesians and what was its significance?

Each time Paul listed what he prayed for, he mentioned what he hoped the Ephesians would receive from God. Note each of the prayers and what he hoped the result would be from that request (vv. 17-19).

What was significant about God's power as Paul described it?

Old Testament Links

The ideas of adoption and being a treasure of God were present in the Old Testament, however Paul took those ideas and expanded them to not only apply to Jews but also to Gentiles. The grace that Jesus introduced to the world changed the understanding of the new life that God offered. Note the differences between the Old Testament passages and the grace offered in Ephesians as you consider these questions.

Read Deuteronomy 4:37-38, 7:7-9, 14:1-2 and Ezekiel 36:25-29. What are the similarities and differences between the passages and Ephesians 1:1-14?

How did Jeremiah 13:11 echo the purpose of God's plans indicated in verses 5 and 6?

In Joel 2:28-29, the prophet foretold the Holy Spirit coming on God's people. What else in the Ephesians passage did it foretell?

Application

How does your position "in Christ," as Paul described in this passage, guide your understanding of a believer's relationship with God?

Paul prayed that the Ephesians would know "the incomparably great power for us who believe." How familiar are you with God's power? Describe how you have seen its result in your life.

Session 2: Grace and Unity

Ephesians 2:1-22

Opening

Consider a tree or flower that begins to die. How is it different from when it was vital and full of life?

Grace may be defined as "God's unmerited favor" and also "God's power which works to regenerate, or sanctify, us." How do these two definitions differ and yet complement each other?

It is by grace, this chapter says, that the Ephesians were saved and made co-heirs, working alongside Christ in this new kingdom. The same grace was bestowed upon each of Christ's followers, or brothers and sisters. The text continued with the illustration of a single house where Jews and Gentiles are side by side. So, it is not only with Christ, but with the joining of the old and the new people of God that they, and consequently we, were united to be a dwelling for his Spirit. As a temple of God, we too have been set apart to work with him for his purposes.

Read Ephesians 2:1-22.

Reading Questions

Describe the spiritual death that Paul named as the state of people according to verses 1-3?

How did that state change because of God's love?

Grace was mentioned three times in four verses of this passage. What are the key points Paul makes about grace?

How are the works contrasted to each other in verses 9 and 10?

Describe how God intended to reconcile the two groups, circumcised and uncircumcised.

Why is it that "you were separate from Christ, excluded from citizenship", according to the first two chapters of Ephesians?

Old Testament Links

The power that raised Christ from the dead also raised you from the dead. The power that saved the Israelites from slavery also saved you from slavery to sin and death. The power that created the universe also transformed your heart from stone to flesh. God has consistently used his power for the benefit of his people. Note the relationship that is pictured within these Old Testament passages as you respond to the questions.

As you read Deuteronomy 9:4-6 and 30:6, 15-20, consider why God saved the Israelites from their enemies and what his ultimate objective in saving them was, particularly in light of the themes found in Ephesians Chapter 2.

How does Deuteronomy 10:14-22 present the idea of dwelling together compared to Ephesians 2:14-22?

Application

What good works have you done lately? Are they an effort at earning Christ's acceptance and love or are they an expression of gratitude for his grace? Perhaps there is a sliding scale of how much we try to earn God's approval and how much we are grateful. Where would your actions fit on a scale of 1 (earning) to 10 (grateful).

God's vision of "one new humanity" challenges us to make unity a central theme of our lives. What kinds of unifying actions have you undertaken in the last few months? How are you helping bring people together? What could you do while walking forward in Christ to make unity a priority?

Session 3: Mystery Revealed

Ephesians 3:1-21

Opening

How would you describe a union, or being united with a group or person? How close do they need to be to fulfill the definition? Share some examples.

Who are the most powerful people in your life? Consider work and home life as well as community and church, (people such as a boss at work, a successful business owner you know, or a local government official). How do they use the power they have?

Paul continued the theme of unity through this chapter, emphasizing the union of God's people further. Unity seems to imply effort is required to join two disparate parts in some way. God too has expended effort and continues to do so today to unite us with himself. This is a key concept in the gospel of Christ. His life, death, and resurrection forgave us for our sins so that we may be reunited with the Father. Unity of God's people to himself is one part of an ongoing process of uniting all his people to one another, as Paul urged in this letter.

Read Ephesians 3:1–21.

Reading Questions

Paul described the "mystery revealed" in verses 6 and 9, the unity of Jews and Gentiles in Christ. What were the three parts of the mystery that Paul described (v. 6)?

What intention did Paul describe behind God's revelation of this mystery?

What are the conditions Paul gave to approach God "with freedom and confidence"?

In prayer, what reasons did Paul give for needing God's power?

What does it mean to be "filled to the measure of the fullness of God"?

God's power was mentioned three times in the prayer that Paul prays for the Ephesians in this chapter. How were these three references tied together in the life of the believer?

Old Testament Links

Paul urged the people of Ephesus toward unity, while also invoking the Holy Spirit to guide them. Perhaps he was saying that unity was going to be possible only through the Spirit. The Holy Spirit's interactions with God's people changed over the two testaments. In the Old Testament, the Holy Spirit dwelt upon a specific person for a specific task. The New Testament shows us that the Spirit is found to dwell within each person all the time. This change in the indwelling of the Spirit was foretold and described in various ways through the Old Testament. Consider this difference as you review the passages for this session.

Isaiah 19:23-25 and Zechariah 2:10-12 prophesied of the united people of God. How did Paul take the unity a step farther than these verses, particularly in relation to the three parts of the mystery revealed (question above)?

What is the Spirit associated with in Micah 3:8 and Ezekiel 36:26-27 and how is that affirmed in this passage of Ephesians?

Application

Paul prayed that the Ephesians would know the love of God - how wide, long, high, and deep it is. What metaphor would you use to describe God's love?

Verse 20 is frequently quoted when we face difficulties. However, the verse also describes a limitation: "power that is at work within us." How great is his power at work within you?

Session 4: Walk Worthy of the Call

Ephesians 4:1-16

Opening

What are the signs of maturity or rites of passage for your family or community?

What resources do you use to prepare for or get equipped for a new project or job?

In this chapter Paul's call for unity in Christ moved toward recognizing that unity did not mean uniformity. Christ gave gifts for individuals, apportioned for each one. These gifts were for building up the one body that each would mature in faith. With both the one and the individual, Paul seemed to imply this would bring growth.

Read Ephesians 4:1-16.

Reading Questions

Paul urged the Ephesians to live worthy, or becoming of, a person called by Christ. What characteristics did that include?

Paul described many "ones" for followers of Christ. Choose two to describe the idea of "one" (i.e.: describe one body or one baptism, etc.).

How did Paul contrast the unity and individuality of those called (vv. 4-6 and 7-13)?

What leadership roles did Christ give to his body? What was the ultimate purpose of these gifts?

What were two traits of infants in the faith and two signs of maturity?

Old Testament Links

Paul's emphasis on Christ's apportionment of gifts stemmed from the Old Testament when the Holy Spirit came upon those who received gifts. That idea continued in the New Testament, but now the Spirit dwells as opposed to spending only a finite period of time with a person. The gifts are representative of Christ and the Spirit and his activity in us.

Ephesians 4:8 and the subsequent two verses come from Psalm 68:18. Describe the ascending and descending that Christ did. The image here is of a conqueror with plunder and tributes in turn given as gifts to those who fought with him or her. What is the implication of Christ as conqueror?

The list of gifts in verse 11 consisted of work that people in the Old Testament as well had done. Note the encouragement and warnings to the people who carried out the work in these passages: 1 Samuel 3:10-11, 19-21; Isaiah 52:7; Ezekiel 34:1-6.

Application

When reading passages like this, it is tempting to strive to "do better." Rather than striving to mature, what can you do? Remember the truths from Chapters 1-3 as well as this chapter.

Ephesians 4:7 says that each has been apportioned gifts, or grace, from Christ. What gift or gifts have you been given? How are you using them to build up the body of Christ and become mature?

Session 5: Put Off the Old Self

Ephesians 4:17-5:2

Opening

How often are you tempted to tell "little white lies", perhaps to keep from hurting someone's feelings? How often do you hear them and how do you respond to them?

What are behaviors that you engaged in or found acceptable before knowing Christ that you find unappealing now?

Paul encouraged believers to create habits of "good works" and "good behavior", while not ignoring that God's grace was the reason for the relationship. The focus on changes to behavior are the result of the relationship with God and the grace received and discussed in the previous chapters.

Read Ephesians 4:17–5:2.

Reading Questions

How did Gentiles live in futile thinking?

How did Paul describe the new way of living coming to the Ephesians?

How was one made new according to verse 23? Describe the new self he mentioned in verse 24.

What activities did it seem the Ephesians were engaging in that Paul disapproved of?

List at least four behaviors that Paul said must be "put off" and the alternate that should be "put on" by the Ephesian believers.

Given the context of verse 30, what did Paul imply was meant by "grieving the Spirit"?

Old Testament Links

The idea of living differently in order to honor God wasn't new for those familiar with the Scriptures. God offered instruction throughout the Old Testament about how to set oneself apart. Note the similarities in the culture of the time to today and what people may have been concerned with given those instructions.

Paul spent time exhorting the Ephesians to "put off" their old selves. After reading Zechariah 8:15-17 and Proverbs 11:12-19, 15:1-6, compare the instruction for Old Testament readers and the Ephesians in following this idea of not living "as the Gentiles do."

Ezekiel 20:40-41 expand upon the "pleasing aroma" metaphor of following God as our example. How is this metaphor extended in Ephesians 5:1-2?

Application

Paul contrasted the "futility of thinking" with the "attitude of the mind." What is your present "attitude of the mind" and how does that attitude impact your thinking? How does that attitude impact your understanding of God's ways and man's ways?

Brainstorm additional adjectives to describe the kind of "talk" that should "come out of your mouths." Looking back on the week, what percentage of your talk was as Paul encouraged? What situations or emotions made it more difficult to be wholesome in speech?

Session 6: Living as Christians

Ephesians 5:3-20

Opening

Ancient text often listed vices in their discussions, as Paul did in today's reading. What vices would you list as prevalent in today's society?

Some vices make for excellent businesspeople, others only hinder relationships. What characteristics would you look for in a partner? Consider a partner of life, of business, of church or charitable events, or any other types.

Paul contrasted the light and dark, wise and unwise, holy and unholy in this passage. The contrasts are easy to outline on paper, but the reality of living it out among people is different. Many people hide their thoughts and actions which would help us understand who they are and if they are "children of the light." Consider the passage personally rather than as an indictment of others to fully appreciate the contrast within ourselves and any area God may want to make changes.

Read Ephesians 5:3-20.

Reading Questions

This passage opens with a list of behavior. For whom is the behavior improper?

What is offered as a suggestion to counteract these behaviors?

What is the consequence of the behaviors summarized in verse 5?

Contrast the works of the darkness and the light according to Paul in verses 8-13.

Verses 15-18 each offer a recommendation on how to walk worthy. What are those suggestions?

What signs did Paul list of the Spirit's presence?

Old Testament Links

As Christians, we know from the New Testament that we have been saved by faith and not works or our behavior. The emphasis on behavior rather than faith points toward the visible changes or differences that a relationship with God has upon a person. We hold David in high esteem as a "man after God's own heart" because much of his life story is about how he lived the way God wanted (works/behavior). However, we also know that he had faith in God, and see in hindsight this is why he was well regarded. The behavior was a reflection of the relationship David had with God.

Ephesians 15:14 is a quote from an unclear source. Some say it is paraphrased from Isaiah 60:1 or Daniel 12:2 while others claim it from poetry or other sources of the time. Consider why some scholars would think so and others argue the opposite.

Psalm 15:1-5, assumed to be one of David's writings, offers a view into the Old Testament ideals of goodness, righteousness, and truth. How is that passage similar to Paul's points in Ephesians 5:3-20?

Application

Recall the last time that you carried something out in secret. How fruitful did it turn out? What would you do differently today compared to that experience?

Paul exhorts the Ephesians to speak to one another with psalms, hymns, and songs from the Spirit. How often and with whom do you speak in this way? How could you do so more often?

Session 7: Living in Family

Ephesians 5:21-6:9

Opening

There is a general idea in coaching and counseling that indicates that struggles create growth. What relationships cause the most struggle in your life?

What are an individual's conditions which make it more challenging to be well in a relationship? Consider emotions, physical condition, history with each other.

There was an emphasis on unity and living as Christ followers throughout the book of Ephesians. Now Paul turned to the closer relationships that we have - family and work. Paul addressed not only the power in relationships, but also used God's example throughout the passage. Readers in Ephesus would have kept the ideas of unity and Christian behavior in mind as applying to this passage as well.

Read Ephesians 5:21-6:9.

Reading Questions

Who submits to whom in the beginning of the passage, verse 21? Give examples. Who has greater authority or power?

Break down the analogy of husband and wife given in verses 22-33. When describing characteristics, consider the first chapters of the letter Ephesians and God's purpose of unity.

The wife is parallel to _____, and some of her characteristics are:

The husband is parallel to _____,
and some of the husband's characteristics are:

How would you describe the interaction between these two
parts?

How do verses 6:1-4 reflect the directions given in verse 5:21?

According to Paul, who is the head of workers and leaders? What
are the instructions given?

Old Testament Links

Relationship with God is the reason for Christ's birth,
life, death, and resurrection. He came that we might
have relationship with God. That relationship is described
throughout the Bible in many ways, but often as family: God

as Father, Jesus as brother, and so on. This topic is clearly an important one to God. Consider how his relationship with us was presented and how loved we are as you read these passages.

God's bride is described in Ezekiel 16:8-14. How does this compare to Ephesians 5:25-27?

Leviticus 19:9-18 gives various laws about corporate life and life with God. How are these laws reflected in Paul's instructions regarding relationships?

Application

Falling into a trap of legalism in relationships is a real temptation. How does God's purpose of unity help in the balance of equality and authority Paul presented?

In the previous chapter, God's love was a key idea Paul presented. How can we pour out that love to others in relationship, as described in this chapter?

Session 8: Walk as Warfare

Ephesians 6:10-24

Opening

In sports or other competitions, we often build up one rival in particular. What rivalry is most prevalent in your local culture or was in your past? What impact did the rivalry have on morale when there was a win? Or a loss?

War is usually defined as taking up arms against an enemy and moving in aggression. However, war may be a "cold" one and could be defined by divisions and conflict instead. What topics divide people today and discussion of them causes conflict and defensiveness?

Paul addressed evil in the world in this passage. Interestingly, he did not speak of the attacks between the groups of good and evil, but rather he focused on the defensive position of believers against evil. This focus served to remind his readers that God has already won the war that is waged, though they continued to live through the battles. The closing of the letter again reminded the readers to live in peace, love, and grace, fearlessly. We are called to do the same.

Read Ephesians 6:10-24.

Reading Questions

Who is the enemy of believers that Paul named? How are they described?

Verses 13-14 repeat the word stand three times. What does that say of the position or activity of the believer in this warfare?

Metaphorically, what do each of the pieces of armor protect against? (i.e.: not only head, but mind)

Belt

Breastplate

Boots

Shield

Helmet

In what two ways does the Spirit help in this battle? How does the believer work with the Spirit in battle?

How did Paul bless the Ephesians at the end of his letter to them?

Old Testament Links

The New Testament tends to cite enemies that are not physically present, aside from the Romans. The ideas of armor are found in Isaiah (11:5, 52:7, 59:17), yet the victory of God is the focus of this passage. The Old Testament presents many enemies of God's people and their battles. When his people faced enemies, God was often involved in the battle and influential in the outcome, just as he was in the New Testament and is still today in the struggles we face. Note the victorious language as you read the following passages.

Evil forces were referenced in Ephesians 6:12; how were these forces fought according to the following verses: Exodus 12:12, 14:14-28, 17:10-15, 2 Samuel 5:22-25, 2 Kings 6:15-17?

What methods were used to stand firm (v. 13-14) in battle in 2 Chronicles 20:15-24 and in Daniel 10:10-21?

Paul closed with an idea from Exodus 20:6. How is this promise expanded by Paul's closing?

Application

Consider the defense that is offered by each of the pieces of armor you listed above. Which do you find is your weakest defense? Write a prayer to God for strength and growth in that area.

What are the hard fights of your day-to-day walk in this season of life? How do you see God fighting for you in this difficulty?

Conclusion

The book of Ephesians is full of truths of life in Christ. From who we are to how we should conduct ourselves, Paul offers insights and practicalities for believers. Note here the main themes of the book of Ephesians.

What did you learn about God?

What did you learn about yourself?

Do you believe that Jesus is the Messiah, the Son of God, and have you received life in his name? If so, describe the qualities of that life.

If this is the first time that you have answered yes to the call of following Jesus, please reach out to a local church or the author to share of your choice and find support for your new life.

To continue your deep dive into "The Old Testament in the Epistles", pick up *James: Know God's Wisdom* to continue your study. Find it at your nearest retailer by scanning the QR code today.

*Order James
Today*

About the Author

Sarah K. Howley is a Bible teacher, passionate about helping believers grow spiritually and take on the character of Christ. She is the founder of InspiritEncourage, an author, speaker, and trained Christian counselor. She has lived in over five countries on four continents and takes her own espresso wherever she goes. Sarah and her husband support initiatives for feeding the hungry and for expanding access to reading.

You can find Sarah on Facebook and Instagram @inspiritencourage. To book Sarah as a speaker at your next event, please contact her through her website. For weekly encouragement and information on her latest releases, sign up for Sarah's newsletter at InspiritEncourage.com.

InspiritEncourage

Also By Sarah K. Howley

Women of the Old Testament Bible Studies
Hope: A Bible Study of Women in Jesus' Lineage
Faith (coming 2025)
Love (coming 2025)

Alive Again Bible Study on Forgiveness
Alive Again: Find Healing in in Forgiveness
Alive Again Bible Study: Find Healing in Forgiveness
Alive Again Forgiveness Prayer Journal

The Son Reveals the Father
I Am: An 8-Session Study of John
Heart: A 12-Session Study of Luke
Word: An 11-Session Study of Matthew
King: An 8-Session Study of Mark

Made in United States
Cleveland, OH
31 January 2025